# MEET
# JESSE JACKSON

MELODY S. MIS

**PowerKiDS**
press

New York

Published in 2008 by The Rosen Publishing Group, Inc.
29 East 21st Street, New York, NY 10010

First Edition

Editors: Nicole Pristash and Jennifer Way
Book Design: Julio Gil
Photo Researcher: Nicole Pristash

Photo Credits: Cover, back cover, title page, headers, pp. 5, 7, 17, 21 © Getty Images; pp. 9, 11, 15, 19 © Associated Press; p. 13 © Michael Mauney/Getty Images.

Library of Congress Cataloging-in-Publication Data

Mis, Melody S.
  Meet Jesse Jackson / by Melody S. Mis. — 1st ed.
      p. cm. — (Civil rights leaders)
  Includes bibliographical references and index.
  ISBN 978-1-4042-4212-8 (library binding)
  1. Jackson, Jesse, 1941– —Juvenile literature. 2. African Americans—Biography—Juvenile literature. 3. Civil rights workers—United States—Biography—Juvenile literature. 4. Presidential candidates—United States—Biography—Juvenile literature. I. Title.
  E185.97.J25M57 2008
  973.927092—dc22
  [B]
                                                  2007034699

Manufactured in the United States of America

# Contents

Jesse Jackson is an important leader. He became part of the **civil rights movement** at a young age. He worked with civil rights leader Martin Luther King Jr. during a time of segregation. Segregation meant that African Americans were kept apart from white people. Blacks did not have the same rights that white people had. Jackson helped change that.

During his life, Jackson formed many groups to help African Americans. He believed blacks and other **minorities** should get good jobs, schooling, and housing. Jackson has spent his life trying to help members of minority groups better their life.

During the 1950s and 1960s, African Americans struggled to get equal rights. They held marches against segregation and unfair laws. This period of time is known as the civil rights movement.

Jesse Jackson believes people are the main cause of change.
He feels that every person can help make the world a better place.

Jesse Burns Jackson was born on October 8, 1941, in Greenville, South Carolina. In 1943, his mother married Charles Jackson, who **adopted** young Jesse. Jackson and his family lived in a poor African-American community. During segregation, blacks could not live in white neighborhoods.

When Jackson was a child, his grandmother gave him books to read so he could learn about the world. She told him that if he studied hard, he could be an important person. Jackson decided he wanted to be a minister. A minister is a person who leads church services.

Segregation laws said that African Americans could not go to white schools. African Americans could not use many of the same public places that whites used. Blacks also had to sit in the back of buses. If a bus became full, they had to give up their seats to whites.

This man is drinking from a water jug that only blacks can drink from.

Jackson was a good student. In high school, he was a star baseball and football player. A national baseball team tried to sign Jackson, but he wanted to go to **college** instead. He got a football **scholarship** to the University of Illinois. He left Illinois after one year and went to North Carolina A&T University. While he was there, he became a part of the civil rights movement. He led **protest** marches and **sit-ins** against segregation.

In 1962, Jackson married Jackie Brown, whom he had met at North Carolina A&T. They had five children.

Sit-ins were a way of protesting segregation in public places. African Americans would go into a white area of a business and sit down. Owners would ask them to leave, but they would not get up.

In 1964, some African Americans held a sit-in at a lunchroom in Georgia, shown here. They felt that they should have the right to be served food, just like whites.

Jackson finished college in 1964. He moved to Chicago, where he studied to become a minister. The following year, Jackson went to a protest march in Alabama. There he met civil rights leader Martin Luther King Jr. King was leading the march to protest segregation and unfair voting laws. At that time, whites in the South made it hard for blacks to vote. King was Jackson's hero because he stood up for blacks.

Jackson became a part of King's civil rights group. King wanted to take the civil rights movement to the North. He asked Jackson to lead the struggle for equality in Chicago. Jackson agreed.

Together, Jesse Jackson (left) and Martin Luther King Jr. (right) helped many African Americans gain equality in Chicago and other parts of the United States.

In 1966, Jackson quit studying to be a minister to lead the Chicago Freedom Movement. Many blacks lived in old, crowded apartment buildings. They were not allowed to rent or to buy homes in white areas. Jackson led protests against this. At last, the city promised to stop treating blacks unfairly.

Jackson was then put in charge of a **program** called Operation Breadbasket. Many Chicago companies sold goods to blacks, but the companies would not let them work there. Operation Breadbasket used **boycotts** to force companies to allow blacks to work for them.

One of the programs Operation Breadbasket started is called Black Expo. One thing the Black Expo does is present goods made by African-American-owned companies. The Black Expo has become a yearly event in many cities.

12

Jesse Jackson is a great speaker. His strong voice and his words have changed many people's beliefs and views.

# Operation PUSH

In 1971, Jackson started a program called People United to Serve Humanity (PUSH). It helped blacks get jobs and start businesses. Jackson believed blacks should have the same chances in business as whites.

PUSH **encouraged** companies to let blacks work for them and to buy goods from businesses owned by blacks. If companies refused, PUSH led boycotts against them. PUSH worked to get blacks to vote in **elections**, too. Jackson believed their votes could decide who would win elections. He made blacks see that they were an important part of the community.

One of Operation PUSH's programs was called PUSH-Excel. It was formed to help young African Americans stay in school. To stay in the program, students had to promise they would study two hours every night.

In 1972, Jesse Jackson spoke to a group of workers in Florida. He told the crowd he wanted to get eight million blacks to sign up to vote!

During the 1980s, Jackson decided to run for president of the United States. To help him with his campaign, or plan, he formed the Rainbow **Coalition**. He gave it that name because there were people of all races in it. There were other minorities too, such as small farmers and working mothers. These were people who did not believe the government cared about them.

The purpose of the Rainbow Coalition was to help Jackson raise money for his campaign. He hoped the group would encourage more minorities to vote for him. Today, the Rainbow/PUSH Coalition works to help minorities get better jobs, housing, and schooling.

The Rainbow/PUSH Coalition has helped people of all races and backgrounds, such as women, workers, and minorities.

17

# Jackson Runs for President

Jackson believed it was possible for an African American to become president of the United States. He hoped to be the first African American elected. In 1984, Jackson ran for president for the first time. He lost, though, and Ronald Reagan was elected instead.

In 1988, Jackson ran for president again. Many people wanted him to win because they liked his campaign speeches. Jackson promised better housing and more programs to help the poor. Jackson lost the election, but his ideas won people over. His success encouraged other African Americans to run for public office as well.

Jesse Jackson's ideas drew in people of all ages and backgrounds.
He is shown here at one of his campaign parties in 1984.

After the 1988 election, Jackson moved to Washington, D.C. He helped with Bill Clinton's presidential campaign. After Clinton won in 1992, he wanted Jackson to go to Africa to talk about peace and **democracy**.

Jackson went to South Africa in 1994. His job was to watch over the elections. At that time, South Africa was segregated and ruled by whites. The election was important because a black man was running for president. His name was Nelson Mandela. Jackson and his team made sure the election was fair and peaceful. Mandela won and he ended segregation in South Africa.

Jackson has freed many Americans who were being held as prisoners in other countries. He did this by going to those countries and talking with their leaders.

In 2002, Jesse Jackson (right) visited Palestine in the Middle East. He encouraged leaders, such as Yasser Arafat (left), to use nonviolent protests to gain peace.

Jackson has won many honors for his work. He won the Chicago Medal of Merit for freeing Americans held in Yugoslavia. He also received the Presidential Medal of Freedom. This is one of the nation's highest honors.

Jackson continues to work for peace and equal rights. He gives speeches and writes about what people and the government can do to help those in need. Jackson has showed Americans the problems minorities and poor people have. He has also been a major force in getting blacks to vote. Jackson will always be known as a great leader in the struggle for equal rights around the world.

**adopted** (uh-DOP-ted)  To have raised a child who has another mother or father.

**boycotts** (BOY-kots)  Joining others in refusing to buy from or deal with a business.

**civil rights movement** (SIH-vul RYTS MOOV-mint)  People and groups working together to win freedom and equality for all.

**college** (KOL-ij)  A school one can go to after high school.

**democracy** (dih-MAH-kruh-see)  A government that is run by the people who live under it.

**elections** (ee-LEK-shunz)  Choosing someone for a position by voting for him or her.

**encouraged** (en-KUR-ijd)  To have given someone a reason to do something.

**minorities** (my-NOR-ih-teez)  Groups of people who are in some way different from the larger group.

**program** (PROH-gram)  A plan for doing something.

**protest** (PROH-test)  To object to or disagree with something.

**scholarship** (SKAH-lur-ship)  Money that helps pay for a person to go to school.

**sit-ins** (SIT-inz)  Acts of protest at which groups of black people refuse to move out of a white-only part of a public place.

# Index

# Web Sites

Due to the changing nature of Internet links, PowerKids Press has developed an online list of Web sites related to the subject of this book. This site is updated regularly. Please use this link to access the list:
www.powerkidslinks.com/crl/jesse/